# THE DAY I MET YOU

**KARTU SUTAR**

This book is dedicated to my family and all my beloved ones, who have always supported me to follow my dreams. This book resembles many moments I witnessed in my life and I am just trying to showcase a handful of them.

# Contents

# Preface

Before you turn the first page, here's something truly unique. For the first time in history, a book comes alive with its own official song—crafted to capture the soul of this journey. Scan the barcode below, listen, and let the music guide you into the world of this story like never before.

Join this journey with us on social media, share your thoughts, and be a part of something special. Don't just read—experience it!

Join Our Journey with our social media platforms:

- **as_seen_by_the_rest_00** and **k_a_r_t_u_23**
- **www.youtube.com/@akhilalmatti7098**

# Acknowledgements

My life is all about my family and my friends. My every work, my every action is all concerned about them. Aaj me jo kuch hu bas unke wajhe se hu. I always wanted to convey my gratitude towards them but I was never able to do so. But today, I can share my message, My gratitude for being part of my journey.

I want to start with **myMom.** More than a mother-son relationship, Our bond is like a best friend's. I always love to share my daily pieces of life stuff with my mom. I never said in front of you but I always love you, Mom. You are my biggest reason to be happy in my life. I literally have no words to explain my feelings.

Next, I want to present my gratitude to my inspiration, **My Dad.** Ek middle class family ke Khwaabo ke bare me mere papa se behetar koi nahi samjh payega. His life starts with his family and ends with his family. He always works so hard just to fulfill our dreams. But whenever we used to ask about his dreams, he always says "When you children grow up and get settled in your life, I just want to go back to my village and want to live my remaining life with peace and happiness.". That's what simplicity means for him. I was never able to tell in front of you Dad, But today I feel like Aapko gale lagake kahu I'm really lucky, and I feel proud to be called the son of *Mr. Sudam P Sutar.* Love you sooooo much, Dad.

We usually say that ek bhai behan ka Rishta ek Chuhe Billi Se Kam Nahi Hota. Off course, even me and my dear sister **Sonu** belong to that same category. But I want to admit today, the maturity she has at her age of just 20, I have never been so. The way she guided me and supported me in my bad times, The word *Thank you* is way too short to express my gratitude. Kabhi Kabhi lagata hai ghar me Sabse Chota Me Hu. The way we share our emotions with each other, It just like we are best friends forever. I am sure even our parents feel proud to watch out for how mature their children are. I ALWAYS LOVE YOU, SONU. You are the best younger sister I ever got in my life.

Friends are always called the backbone of any new start. I have always being an introverted person. Limited people, limited friends, and limited happiness. But a person who knows me very well is my dear friend, **Rakesh Koppad**. We have been friends since our childhood. We both have some awesome memories together and I praise that every time I remember. But today I want to tell you, my friend, I always love you and I am thankful to help me out with the craziest time I ever faced.

Next, she is the person who always supported my work and my passion for writing this novel. The way she praises me and being dedicated to our bounding is beyond the limits. As a younger sister, she always loves to stay connected with me and Rakesh since our school times. When I began this journey, she was the 1st person to know, and she was the first person to support.

If you are reading this, yes, I am talking about you, my dear sister. **Preeti**. Thanks to be kind and soo soo supportive of my work and my life. You always remains my special person thoughtout my life.

**Ishu**. I love to call you by this name. You are the one who helped me to overcome my anxiety. My past shattered me away but you picked me up to settle down to my original personality. After all, you are my childhood friend who knows me very well and also knows how to add happiness to my life.

Next, you are my inspiration for my work *Akhil Anna*. I still remember when I first met you with the partial lyrics that I have written and made you to listen it. Your 1st expression was "It's awesome. Let's work on this". And now, here we are. Such a sensational composition and voice you added to my song. I am so grateful to have you, Anna. The journey that we witnessed was meant to be a memorable roller coaster ride.

*Navithma.* My first foreign friend I ever get connected to. We connected through my Instagram page and we got used to share our ideas. And you won't believe it's been 4 years now that we are best friends. You always showed a special interest in my work, and that's why I not only praise you but also loved to spend time with you. Thank you so much, yaar.

A sensational singer from our SGBIT College, *Nandita Mathad.* It took me two months just to get in touch with you and offer you to sing a song for me. I never felt like I was talking with you for the first time because you are so sweet and humble. I was on a journey with you to discover myself. The way you understood my feelings was really meant a lot to me. I am sure this song will be one of our finest works ever, and I appreciate everything you have done for me.

I was always thankful to the person who always helped me to progress in our own way and who always stands like a protective backbone in our college. Our beloved HOD *Mr. Rajendra Galagali.* They always supported and encouraged me to write my novel and publish it. My heart is full of gratitude to you sir.

*Abhishek Patil.* Also known as *Mr. patil.* I never admitted it in front of him, but I want to tell you bhai, you are my life guider. The struggle that I am having in

Bangalore, You are the only one who keeps me guiding to overcome the obstacles and fight for myslef. I want to admit that I went through many people in my life but never got a friend like you. I always love you, Bhai.

***Pramod Dalavi and Kiran Nakadi.*** These two people will be my lifeline for any solution I needed in my life. Our roads of life might be busy with our profession, but we always believe for that one moment to meet together and have some quality time.

And last but not least, I want to thank ***Vinod Kolkar,*** who always led my way when I first entered my degree college. We had spended some awesome days, bro.

I want to thank ***Ganesh Bhai and Ruturaj,*** who always filled my life with happiness and joy. I hope to meet you soon.

I want to thank my beloved sister, ***Prabha.*** You are so kind and sweet who not only helped me out to improve my work but also guided me to work efficiently. I really hope we meet as soon as possible.

I want to thank my beloved juniors ***Shrinidhi, Khushi, Chaitali andSaniya Malik,*** who are always excited to help me to promote my book and my work. You people always helped me when I needed it. I love you all.

I want to thank my dear sister ***Sanskruti.*** She always vibes with me and my sister Sonu. And yeah, she is always a supporter to me. You always remain my dearest one. Love you soo much, sister.

# Foreword

<u>Kartik Sudam Sutar</u>

Kartu Sutar, also known as Kartik Sudam Sutar is an Indian author, lyrics writer, and a engineer based in Belagavi, Karnataka. He has graduated from S.G Balekundri Institute of Technology, Belagavi, and he is currently working for a Private Company in Banglore. He was always fond of writing small stories in both Kannada and English as well as some Kannada and Hindi songs of his own. In college, he worked on many journals and research papers that were published in academic journals. As this is his first official book publication, this is a significant milestone for him.

# CHAPTER I

# The Broken heart

"Love has been emphasized to be a beautiful feeling in the world, but it gets hallowed without the foundation of truth and honesty".

• • •

Hello there!

I am Kartu, the author of *your* story.

Your Story? Funny right?

Yes. It's your story, where you can relate yourself to your past things. It might be any emotion you suffered or something that you witnessed in the flaws of heavy storms.

But you know what?

Sometimes, you have to walk a long way to get rid of your past.

But, it always draws you back to where it all began with a small piece of emotion. Isn't It?.

So, this story is all about love, honesty, and betrayal.

Relatable to this, Hindi me Ek kahawat hai,

"Andhero me chale Musafir ke har Raha mai Ek nayi umeedo ka jaha hota hai."

I still remember the day. It's 16$^{th}$ of October that is still etched in my memory, as vivid as the day it happened. It was the day, that my dear friend Karan faced the ultimate test of his loyalty. Ravi was his closest confidant who always used to be with him to fight any flaws he suffered.

Finally, in the blink of an eye, she appeared. The girl with curly hair and a thin face, who had once been the reason for Karan's happiness, now stood before him with another man. As Karan looked at her, a hidden regret tugged into his heartstrings.

Karan: Hey.

Gayatri: Hmm.

She muttered, casting a cold and dismissive glance his way. Karan could see how impolite she was being.

Karan: Sorry for the last week. I didn't mean to call or text you when I was drunk. Umm I...

Karan hesitates, trying to make amends.

Gayatri: I know. It didn't surprise me at all, and guess what? I want to introduce someone that *you must know*.

Gayatri replied, her tone dripping with sarcasm. Karan wasn't surprised by her words, as Ravi had prepared him for what was coming next.

Karan: Okay, go ahead.

Gayatri: let me introduce you to my boyfriend, Abhishek. He is studying at New Drek University in Delhi, and you know what, he's being really nice to me compared to a person who...

let it be. I don't want to talk about it.

Her words hit Karan like a ton of bricks, causing him to crumble inwardly, but he tried to keep his composure despite the pain he felt.

Karan: Abhishek.

As he knew Karan was bringing up the point, Abhishek's gaze was gentle.

Abhishek: Yes, Bhai.

Karan politely states.

Karan: Abhishek, even though we had our past filled with problems, she is still an adorable girl, Just like a small child. She loves to have someone by her side who will enjoys every moment with her. Her sole desires were love and happiness, which I could not fulfill for her. So, the only favor I want from you is that you be the one to play the role of caretaker and make her dreams come true. That's all I wish for. Besides, I know you'll take good care of her.

There was a moment of silence before Abhishek spoke. His words were laced with sincerity.

Abhishek: Bhai, I have heard a lot about you from my friends, about how wise and humble your personality is. I know you're a kind and caring person, and I know you had a past with her and I respect that. But now, it's my duty to protect her and shower her with love and happiness.

Gayatri agreed "Of course, he will." affirming her trust in Abhishek's commitment.

Ravi interjected with a cutting remark

Ravi: Yeah, of course, he will. Abhishek, take care of her and ensure she doesn't ditch you for class and money.

*That's a brutal hit.* Ravi nailed it. Abhishek was taken aback, while Gayatri glared at Ravi with furious indignation.

Karan tried to defuse the situation. "Come on yaar Ravi," he said, although he secretly accepted Ravi's concern.

Finally, Karan opened up and shared his sentiments.

Karan: *Anu,* I hope you find happiness and always stay true to your *actual* nature.

He admits, using the nickname he often called her.

His words stirred up a flood of cherished memories in her, prompting her to respond. But instead of responding with the attitude she carried so long at this moment was just able to reply with only one word.

"Umm." she said, feeling a tinge of remorse.

Karan held her gaze, but she couldn't meet his eyes.

The moments dissolved when they had their final adieu. Karan and Ravi took off.

There was a moment of silence when Ravi rode on his bike with Karan. When finally, Karan whispered something.

Karan: Stop the bike.

Immediately Ravi stopped the bike and glanced back at Karan.

Karan couldn't bear it any longer. He had been holding in his emotion for too long, and now, as he stands next to Ravi's bike, he could feel the dam breaking. Karan stumbled onto the nearby sidewalk and sat quietly for a long time.

Ravi holds his shoulder and sits along with him, suggesting him

Ravi: Tere Mann me jo kuch hai use bahar aane de.

Suddenly, Karan buried his face in Ravi's chest, overcome with emotions of extreme pain. Tears streamed down his cheeks as he released a series of heart-wrenching sobs.

• • •

Dear friends, life has lots of ups and downs. A person who was so important in his life is now a reason for his grief.

So let's talk about my friend Karan Chauhan. Despite with his bold and straightforward nature, he also maintained a hard working personality. He also loves to be with his family and a few friends whom he called his comfort people. Deep inside, a little sensitive kind of personality. But still, he is the kind of person who is brave enough and loves to help people in their bad times.

Apart from this, he made an impact with his impressive communication with people and won many awards for his impressive skills. A district-level classic chess champion for two consecutive years is the best example to highlight his glory.

I am sure you will discover many things about him and his past life in this journey.

At last, do you really believe that the person who has never entertained the thought of hurting anyone, even in their dreams, deserves to endure all this suffering?

# CHAPTER II

# New Beginning

Finally, the fateful moment has arrived. Karan is aware that her eyes are about to reveal something that he barely grasps. The moonbeams were privy to this moment of emotion. Even her mind admitted, "This is the moment I have been waiting for. Let me express my sentiments. For if I don't, I may never see you again, *my love*". Her heartbeat quickened, and she made her move.

*"Karan...you know I cannot survive without you. The moments we spent together, were pure bliss."*

She admits once more to herself.

A tear rolled down her cheek, and the scene faded into obscurity.

"Karan, I Lo-..."

Just then, Ravi interjected.

"My apologies for the interruption, Karan. I was here to tell you that they've got into an accident..."

• • •

After Six months ...

Changes can be scary, but do you know what's scarier?

Allowing fear to stop you from growing, evolving, and progressing as an individual human. That's not the new beginning means. Is it?

Hello friends, welcome back! In the previous chapter, you all had a small glimpse of Karan's past. It described how his love and kindness were taken for granted and ruined him. He was broken, shattered like pieces of broken glass. He was *hurt*. As a result of this incident, he lost himself, who used to have interaction with people. And now it's only him who feels the pain for himself.

Whatever he suffered at that point, I'm glad he started focusing on his career even after all that. The only damage was that he was no longer himself.

As social beings, we often get hit by incidents that eradicate us. The matter at lies in the fact is that, regardless of our choice it depends that we reclaim our original forms or not. fate has deemed specific individuals as the ones destined to guide us back to our origins.

But Hold ON, "Picture Abhi Baki hai Mere Dost".

For Karan, there are a lot of twists and turns to face.

SO, LET'S FIND OUT!

• • •

Ravi: Hey, Congratulations buddy!

Ravi exclaimed in excitement

Leaping into action, he threw his arms around Karan's shoulder, embracing him from behind with such force that Karan was about to lose his balance.

Karan: For what?

He asked, wriggling out of Ravi's grasp

Karan: Bhai, mera dum ghut jayega.

Ravi: Didn't you check the college forum? You won the All Elite Speech Competition! You are selected for the national competition now. And do you know the venue?

Karan: Where?

Ravi exclaimed in disbelief.

Ravi: You don't even know that. How did you even get selected? It's in Ooty.

Karan: Oh.

Karan responded non- chalantantly, his expression portraying nothing. Ravi was taken aback.

Ravi: "Oh?" Bhai,Tum khush Nahi Ho?

Karan: Come on, it's not a big deal.

Ravi: Aah ha, come on yaar, you have to cheer up. And you're not getting away with this. If you don't wanna treat me to dinner, Aaise bahane toh mat bana

Karan's face lit up with a playful grin. Having made a playful bet, Karan graciously accepted the terms - *a dinner that Ravi was entitled to.*

Karan: Chill Mere Yaar. Dinner's on me tonight. Khush?

Ravi: That's my boy.

Ravi nodded with astonishment. Then suddenly, Tringgggggggg.........!!!!!! The bell rang.

Ravi: Dude, we are gonna be late!

Karan: Wait. Seriously?

Karan's eyes widened in astonishment as Ravi's words sank in. Ravi shuddered at the thought of facing their strict teacher, who threatened him with severe consequences the last time he was late.

Ravi: Yes, I am. I never dare to miss any of them. Miss Shweta gave me death glares last time. *"Don't you dare miss my lectures or else..."*

Karan nodded with a gentle smile on his face. He reassures Ravi.

Karan: Haha, we better hurry then! Let's not keep Miss Shweta waiting. And don't worry, We'll make it on time buddy.

Ravi nodded. Despite Karan being a lone wolf, he knew he could always rely on his longtime friend Ravi for support. The two broke into a sprint. Just as they were about to make it to the door, Ravi stumbled, but Karan quickly caught him.

Ravi: Thanks, Maccha.

Ravi breathed a sigh of relief, and then his gaze fell upon the object that had caused his near fall - a stunning *blue Valvanight bag.*

Ravi: Wow!

He gasped in amazement. He picked up and exclaimed.

Ravi: *The blue Valvanight.* An American company known for its versatile designs.

Karan nods and then suggests,

Karan: That must be very expensive. Anyway, we really don't have time for this. Someone must've dropped it; we should return it. Let's hand it over to the department. They'll take care of it.

Ravi nodded and both visited the department office to meet Mr. Rajeev who was the head of the department. After handing over the bag to Mr. Rajeev, they hastened to attend Ms. Shweta's lecture but were late by 10 minutes.

"Damn! What an unlucky way to start the day" they admitted.

• • •

It's half past twelve in the afternoon. The campus was abuzz with students rushing to and from classes.

Ravi: Do you think the rightful person has reached out to Mr. Rajeev?

Karan: Let's find out.

Despite the bag's high cost, no one came to retrieve it from the department head. As a precaution, Mr. Rajeev assured them that he would contact them if an inquiry was made about the bag.

Ravi: I didn't have breakfast today. Let's not wait for dinner. Treat me to something from the canteen after we finish the next period.

Karan grinned and nodded.

Karan: Okay fine, let's have something after class.

Two more hours passed away. Karan and Ravi headed to the canteen to have a chill and of course, fill their empty stomachs. As they were about to take a seat, someone yelled, which grabbed their attention along with everyone else present.

***KARAN...!***

It stunned everyone in the canteen when a girl appeared behind them as they turned behind. With mesmerizing hazel eyes and long strands of hair bouncing off her shoulder, this girl looks stunning and lovely. just like "a beautiful sunflower was ready to bloom when the first rays of sunlight fell on it."

The only thing that was wrong with her was that her face was hardened with anger and set with flames. With her first cannonball, she flung herself at Karan.

Girl: "How dare you? Where is it? Where did you two hide it?"

Ravi: Yeeee? Lagata Ise Chad gayi hai ....

Girl: SHUT UP!

At this point, with her death glare, she was ready to finish them off.

Karan stepped forward, looking flustered.

Karan: Sorry? What are you talking about? You...

She interrupted the conversation and yelled

Girl: My bag! The one you stole this morning. Where did you hide it? I want it RIGHT NOW!

Ravi: Uh? What do you mean by stole? We didn't take your bag? We just...

She interrupts again.

Girl: "DON'T PLAY WITH ME!" I saw the whole thing on surveillance footage. You snatched it from the ground and bolted. And now I want it back.

Karan stepped in before it went too far. He said calmly

Karan: You want your bag and an apology, right? Come with me, I'll give it to you.

Ravi and all the others present were surprised by his actions. Karan is known to be a man of action, not diplomacy. Ravi was still trying to figure out why Karan was taking this so calmly and what he meant by an *apology*. They didn't steal the bag.

Karan did not find it interesting to talk further. So he began to walk away.

Girl: Excuse me? Where are you heading?

He turned around and glanced at her.

Karan: Follow me. You will find your answer.

Ravi looks confused, as well as the girl. What was going on in his mind? No explanation was found.

Both of them followed Karan with lots of things going on in their minds... They were taken to the department head. Karan explained to Mr. Rajeev about the situation and requested him to hand over the bag to her. Furthermore, he suggested that the department head to clarify the owner's doubts.

Mr. Rajeev stared straight at the girl, brought the bag from the locker, and solicited to verify if she was the owner. The girl was unsure of what had just happened.

Girl: Yes, sir. It's mine.

Mr. Rajeev: You know what? Karan and Ravi were the ones to pick it up on their way and handed it to me to find the owner this morning. I believe you owe them an apology.

Hearing this, the girl was stunned by silence. Ravi could see guilt was written all over her face and the embarrassment she wore because of the chaos she created a while ago.

Then Ravi had a hint of sarcasm in this tone

Ravi: It seems, Miss... well, whoever you are. I think it's your turn to apologize for your *High-class Drama*.

Girl: I... I'm really sorry for what happened.

As she tried to find the right words to justify her behavior, her mind could not find the right path.

Girl: I'm ashamed of what I did. I know that-..

Karan interrupted her and finally exclaimed his words.

Karan: Hold on. Don't point fingers without knowing the *whole truth*.

He sounded pretty reserved but his attitude still showed politeness.

Karan: Your reckless words revealed your behavior and secondly, you never listened to us. And now you're acting as if you're guilty? Unfortunately, your apologies aren't enough to prevent your rude behavior. We don't need your apology. So, please just leave.

And with that, the conversation came to an end as Karan and Ravi made their exit. Although Ravi was entertained by Karan's stern response, he couldn't help but notice the visible shift in the girl's demeanor before they left. She tucked her hair behind her ear, her face contorting with regret, tears welling up in her eyes. She realized that her actions were wrong and mustered up the courage to make a proper apology, no matter what it cost.

• • •

Nobody knows when you are going to be *Defeated*. Even if you believe you have an advantage in a battle.

But, have you noticed the change of behavior in Karan?

I'm sure you did.

The wounds of his past have plunged him into the depths of darkness, causing him to reveal his sinister side. However, let me assure you, that is not the true essence of

Karan.

I eagerly anticipate the events that will bring about his healing and improvement.

Till then,

This is Kartu, signing off...

Until we meet again.

# CHAPTER III

# Hame Tumase Pyaar Kitna..

*Hame Tumase Pyaar Kitana,*
*Yeh Hum Nahi Janate.*
*Magar Jee Nahi Sakate...*
*Tumare Beena.... Aaaa.*

The pleasant and melodic voice of Kishor Kumar playing on the radio, made both of them feel these vibes, filled with the chilled breeze and fanned out in the beautiful mountains of Galibeedu. Then, she continued.

" Thank you, Karan... You brought me back to the person I used to be. A few years ago, I was lost. But now I'm myself again."

Karan looked at her, a smile playing on his lips.

" You know what Karan, this moment we are witnessing, it just feels like, *Yeh Pal aur ye Lamha mere Zindagi ke haseen palo me se ek hai*"

He nodded with a smile and folded his arms on his chest to recapture the beauty of this evening.

As the song ended, she gazed at Karan, feeling a strange sensation in her chest that she had never felt before. It was as though her heart was bursting with emotions she couldn't quite put her finger on. Suddenly, it dawned on her. "Is this the feeling we experience when we love someone? Am I in love with him?" she whispered to herself, unable to hide the smile that had crept onto her lips. She couldn't help but feel grateful for this moment. She knew that this feeling, this connection that she shared with Karan was something that she wanted to hold onto forever.

*"I... I am in love with him."*

• • •

Ravi: If I am not mistaken, you have selected the Arduino system. Isn't it? What's so interesting about it?

Karan: Yes, I do. I am in love with new technology that helps to improve our daily lives. In Arduino, we can feed any command and also we can use our voice commands to control all the mechanisms.

Ravi: That's interesting.

Karan: I think that even you have acquired sufficient knowledge of traditional machines and operations because of your previous project.

Ravi: Of course. I....

Tringgggggggggggg.......

And just then the bell rang signaling the end of their conversation.

Karan: There it is. Okay, Ravi. Tujhe Shaam Me Miltha Hu, after my Lab. And don't you dare to BUNK YOUR CLASS.

He intentionally avoided it and acted sarcastically.

Ravi: Ahh, Karan. You have your class right?. OMG! You are already late. I think you should leave. I don't want you to be late.

Ravi urges Karan to rush to his next lecture.

Karan: Saale Tuh Kabhi Nahi Sudrega.

He left with his words and urges for his class which is on the 2$^{nd}$ floor. When Karan was a few steps away from the 1$^{st}$ floor, a soft, sweet voice whispered his name.

*"Karan Bhaiya..."*

In a moment of surprise, Karan turned around and exclaimed to himself by looking at her, "Awww... How cute!".

A skinny and delicate cute little girl, with bouncy short hair and eyes that were like moonlight. She looks elegant in her pink frock. Karan's face was poured with a gentle smile, which we haven't seen in the past few months.

Karan: Yes, my cute little angel. What's your name? How can I help you?

Little girl: Hello Bhaiyya. My name is Reeta. And guess what? I have a present for you.

As his eyes widened, he glanced at her and said...

Karan: A present? For me? That's so sweet.

An attractive blue box was handed to him by Reeta as she opened up her classy bag. A fashionable box with a dazzling violet flower design.

Along with that, a letter is attached to the box, with something written on it. When he opened the letter, he found:

" I AM SORRY".

Karan was flustered.

Reeta kept looking at him and then suggested

Reeta: Please open this box.

In a puzzled state of mind, Karan opens up the box. Where he finds out a *recorder*.

"That's strange," Karan said.

With a snoopy mind, he pressed the start button and he was surprised to hear a familiar voice.

"Hello, Karan. I am sorry for what I did when we met last time. I know that it was unfriendly, unprofessional, unethical, Jo bhi ho. But to be honest this grief is killing me like anything. I feel ashamed and miserable for what I did. And I am sure you never allowed me to keep my point and you will walk out. So, this was the only way to express my apology. I hope you get my point. By the way, please turn back. I am waiting for your response."

He chuckled but tried to hide in front of Reeta. As he turned back, he was delighted to see her cute face.

Suddenly, Reeta exclaimed.

Reeta: Chalo, Mera Kaam toh ho gaya. Bye bhaiya...

Like a fragile butterfly, she nudges with peaceful adieu, adorned with a radiant smile that illuminates her demure countenance.

"Thank you, dear" Karan replied by kissing her forehead.

After that, he turned his attention to the girl standing behind him. He couldn't help but feel touched by her sincerity.

With both hands tangled around her ears, she offered her apologies like a small child.

Yes. The girl who fired a thousand cannonballs at him was now standing before him and apologizing in such a unique and cute way.

Karan grins again.

Girl: I hope you accepted my apology.

He shrugged. His expressions were undefined to identify. He remained silent for a few moments before finally speaking.

Karan: Might be. But, in my entire life, I have never been pleased with such a pleasant and lovely apology. So,

She keeps looking at him, peering, obviously expecting something. Karan smiled at her, and said,

"I accept your apology."

She smiled back. Her face was filled with joy, peace, and calmness. She was really glad that her devise actually worked!

Girl: I knew it. I was sure it's gonna work. Thank you for comforting me. I am feeling relaxed now. By the way, I am Naviketana Maheshwari from the 2nd-year Computer Science dept. You can call me Navi.

Karan: Nice to meet you, Navi...

He takes a pause

Karan: I would say this meeting was quite peaceful and lovely in comparison with previous encounters. Isn't it?

She nodded with a smile. "It certainly was," she said. "I'm glad we were able to talk it out civilly this time."

The whole conversation ended with a satisfied nod from both of them. They parted ways with a final adieu for today, feeling relieved that the dispute was over. When the vision has turned away from the scene, the moment can sense the cold breeze of happiness warms up the mind, bringing a sense of calmness.

• • •

In the realm of Naviketana, a captivating young girl who graced the whole college. Her charming demeanor and impeccable style bewitched those around her, captivating all with her attractive beauty. Naviketana possessed an extraordinary memory that earned her fame within the walls of her college. But still, she remains a believer in fairy tales. The kind of personality she builds with, who wishes to please with a constant desire to spread joy and happiness wherever she goes. But on the other side, the gloom of dark clouds always terrorizes her, filled with the horrible past she faced.

There is no doubt that Karan and Naviketana had a path of darkness, but the storylines divide them up on several levels individually. Karan wanted to pursue the path of light, while Naviketana chose to end the shadows of darkness. But despite the differences in their paths, both still remained a believer in fate, believing that even in the darkest of times, joy and happiness can still be found.

But life is all about ups and downs and twists and turns. So, what's next for both? Only time will tell what lies ahead for Karan and Naviketana. But no matter what, they will always remain connected by their faith in fate and the journey that lies ahead. And guess what? There are lots more to come.

Let's find out in chapter 4.

Till then, SEE YA

# CHAPTER IV

# The Genesis of Forged Friendship

Today, this evening is set to witness something that has never happened before. Karan with a smooth spade beard was waiting for someone. His graceful blue suit were a source of amusement and charm.

Finally, his gaze gleamed up when he finds the one he was waiting for.

Her curly and shiny hair were bouncing on her shoulder. When she flips around her beautiful hair, he finds the hidden moon that appeared in front of him that lights up this decent night.

• • •

True friendship blossoms like a vibrant flower forged after a long winter.

True friendship can save you from the verge of darkness where you lean towards being fallen.

True friendship discovers the beauty of honesty and the importance of forgiveness, empathy, and humanity.

Welcome back to the tale of the thousands memories you are going to witness in this journey. I am your co-Piloy Kartu, and we will come up with a new piece of craft to complete this riddle of friendship and love. Let us begin the journey of discovering the untold stories of this realm. We will find joy and sorrow, the laughter of the past, and the cries of the future. This is a *journey of a thousand memories.* Let us begin!

• • •

"Hey, Mr. Karan."

Karan pivoted, to discover Mr. Kaushal Upaydhya gesturing towards him. Standing just behind him as he was about to head towards his next lecture, Mr. Kaushal, his class teacher, sought his attention.

"Good morning, Sir."

Karan nodded with a smile to present his warm greeting to Mr. Kaushal.

Mr. Kaushal: Good Morning Karan, and congratulations for being the winner of all elite competitions and getting selected for the national level.

Karan nodded, a subtle grin spreading across his face.

Karan: Thank you, Mr. Kaushal. I am happy that I have made it through. And Thanks to you, without your help I wouldn't have made it.

Mr. Kaushal: Your diligent work, dedication, and passion have paid off, My boy. Make sure you keep this passion growing in order to improve yourself. It will be your turn to shine among the best out of the best.

Karan's heart swelled with pride as he took in Mr. Kaushal's words.

Karan: Thank you so much, that means a lot.

Mr. Kaushal chuckled. Patting Karan on the back and exclaiming,

Mr. Kaushal: You are really impressive with your technical aspects. So, I am selecting you for the Kaushalya State level Exhibition. I want your talents and skills to be showcased. And this exhibition is the perfect platform for you to do so. So, what do you think?

Karan's mind raced with many thoughts but still, he felt excited about the offer because that's what he liked to do. But the nature of his personality prevented him from expressing his excitement other than a slight smile of agreement.

Karan: Thank you so much, Mr. Kaushal. I promise to give my best shot at winning the competition.

Mr. Kaushal clapped Karan on the back again, a proud smile on his face.

Mr. Kaushal: That's the spirit, my boy! There is no doubt that you will make a significant impact in this competition. So, meet me at my office after lunch. We gonna discuss more about the exhibition.

Karan nodded.

Karan: Sure Mr. Kaushal. Have a great day.

After a newfound sense of determination and the ability to examine himself, Karan walked away and took on the new challenge.

• • •

Ravi: Mr. Kaushal selected you for the state-level exhibition. That's awesome machha.

Ravi was delighted by this news. He continued.

Ravi: Did they inform you what kind of project you're gonna work on?

Seated in the vast outdoors, basking in the present surroundings, Karan calmly stated his opinion about the exhibition.

Karan: He told me to meet after lunch. I am sure they might have some new projects to work on. And..

He paused for a second. The tense look on his face reveals his concern. He takes a deep breath and continues.

Karan: I mean, there will probably be a bunch of people there, who are way better than me. A bit intimidating, to be honest.

Ravi: Ahh, Come on. Don't underestimate yourself, Aur Please, Tujh pe ye suit nahi karta. You are not meant to lose.

You are meant to win. And you know what?

Karan keeps looking at him. Ravi continued. His tone lowered when he made his statement.

Ravi: Jaane kitni ladayi tune khud ladake jeeti hai. Tabhi toh kabhi nahi dare tum. Toh ab kaisa darr?

Karan was taken aback. Karan had witnessed it again, that Ravi was so serious and caring about expressing something that Karan needs right now.

Karan nodded with a grateful smile adorning his face along with Ravi's motivating words. His words filled Karan with determination and courage.

Karan: Thanks, Yaar... Alright then, I will take your advice and make my way to meet Mr. Kaushal.

Ravi exclaimed with excitement

Ravi: That's my boy. Looking forward to hear what you get. Challo shaam me mil aur bata kya baate huwi.

Karan nodded in agreement before saying adieu.

• • •

After being cheered up by Ravi's encouraging words, Karan felt a newfound determination as he headed toward Mr. Kaushal's office. The exhibition was just around the corner, so he needed all the guidance he could get. Taking a deep breath, he knocked on the door and waited for permission to come in. Then, a familiar voice rang out from the office,

Mr. Kaushal: Come in.

Karan entered the room, feeling a mix of nervousness and excitement. Mr. Kaushal gestured for him to take a seat and Karan obliged, setting into a chair across Mr.Kaushal.

Mr. Kaushal: I am glad you could make it. We have a lot to discuss about the exhibition. The committee has just mailed me the guidelines.

Karan nodded attentively, eager to absorb all the information he could. Mr. Kaushal began to explain the rules and regulations of creativity and innovation he must add in this exhibition. Karan's mind buzzed with ideas, eager to make a mark at the upcoming event. Just as he became engrossed in the conversation, a knock on the door interrupted their discussion.

" Excuse me, may I come in?"

His vision is impacted by her voice, which sounded familiar to him.

Mr. Kaushal: Come in. Karan, meet your partner, Miss *Naviketana.*

As Karan looked at Naviketana, his initial reaction and surprise became apparent on his face, while at the same time, a brief flicker of surprise appeared on Naviketana's face. The last time they had met, there had been a misunderstood argument led by Naviketana which left Karan with perplexed and disheartened. However, just when Karan's mind was filled with uncertainty, Navi's genuine remorse had reached him. She later approached him, providing a heartfelt and sincere apology.

The initial reservation between them began to fade, with a warm smile Naviketana extended her hand towards Karan, her eyes filled with anticipation.

"Hello, I am delighted to work with you."

Karan was encouraged by Naviketana's positive response, which was reciprocated by her smile. Karan firmly shook her hand. With their shared vision and complementary abilities, the meeting continued. Karan and Naviketana gleamed off each other's enthusiasm as they discussed their ideas openly. They quickly realized that their strengths complemented each other and the synergy between them was palpable. Finally, the discussion was concluded with Mr. Kaushal's words

" I expect a lot from both of you. In my opinion, this partnership will help improve your skills in a positive way. Make sure to utilize each other's expertise. Got it?

Karan and Naviketana exchanged a glance, their eyes filled with determination to live up to those expectations.

Karan: You can count on us, sir. We both commit to delivering our best performance.

Naviketana nodded in agreement.

Naviketana: I agree with Karan. We won't settle for anything less than excellence.

Mr. Kaushal smiled, pleased with their determination.

Mr. Kaushal: I have faith in you both. Best of luck.

Karan and Naviketana exchanged another glance and nodded with their expressions filled with mutual respect.

• • •

" As we previously decided, we can install AI techniques and lead this project to some extent and...."

When Karan was explaining his strategy for the upcoming exhibition, he finds out Navi gazing out towards the window. When he looks out the window, he finds that it is surrounded by sensational cold weather with a chilled breeze where few squirrels enjoy each other presence. This adoring sight, made her to be disappear from the real world and get lost in her own thoughts. As Navi and Karan sat in the cozy corner of the library, a gentle breeze crept in through the slightly ajar windows. This breeze carried a refreshing coolness. It blew playfully around the room, gently rustling the pages of the books on the nearby shelves. He kept noticing that the subtle touch of the breeze brushed against Navi's cheeks, creating a soothing sensation that seemed to invite relaxation and some past memories to her.

Karan: Sometimes, this cold environment draws people back to some things they used to love in the past.

Snapping back to reality she caught sight of Karan's beaming smile, realizing just how lost she had been in the labyrinth of her own thoughts.

Navi: Oh, I am sorry. Umm. I was illuminated for a while.

She smiled and said,

Navi: But yes, you are right. Kuch toh baat hai inn hawaon me. It just feels like these cold breezes whispers, like, *Remember the moments you once loved and the moments you once lived.*

Reflecting on Navi's words, he finds nothing but to agree with what she had just said. A small glimpse of recollection turned him to the past where he and Anu have lived mesmerizing moments together. But, reality thrashes him back into the present world. He descends himself to his normal form. But Navi's subtle mood led him to explore a new perspective of calmness.

Karan: Well, I never thought of it. But yes, these environments always fascinate people to remember the moments they once lived and loved. And you, have an elegant way of describing the things. I like your new perspective of peace.

Navi nodded with a grateful smile. Playfully she stated.

Navi: I am glad my observation finally resonating with you. But tell me what specifically drew you to appreciate my perspective? Was it the way I observed things?"

Karan: Umm. ahh. Nope.

She exclaimed with curiosity.

Navi: Then what?

Karan: Umm. Actually, It's not about the perspective.

He takes a pause. She keep looking at him, waiting for his response

"then?"

Karan: Its about..... *you,*

Her heart skips a beat. Karan paused again for a moment, gathering his thoughts, before continuing.

Karan: It's about being yourself. You have the ability to be true and straight to people. Which means it impacts every word you say that brings a good sensation of happiness. And believe me, *Har kisime me yeh baat nahi hoti.*

He pointed indirectly to his deteriorating situation but he was quite satisfied with *her* point of happiness. Her expression obliged his beautiful words. A warm blush spread across her cheeks.

Navi: Umm. Thank you, Karan. And you know what?

Karan raises his chin awaiting for her next words.

Navi: When we trust our own instincts, embrace our passion, and stay true to our values, we become the most effective version of ourselves. *Just like you.*

Her words resonated deeply with Karan and he nodded, a satisfied smile spreading across his face. He realized that he had been holding himself back. But now, he can express his feelings in front of her. Navi's openness and authenticity have inspired him to open up to explore himself.

" Umm. I mean. Thank you, Navi."

She smiled back. Grateful for her honesty, they led themselves to prepare well for the upcoming battle and our vision dissolved to travel for the next destiny.

• • •

Navi: So, finally we are here. The past few weeks have added a lot of practice, and now, we are ready to prove ourself. Isn't it.

Karan nods, but there was a trace of nervousness in his eyes. He takes a deep breath, trying to steady his racing heart. Sensing his anxiety, Navi steps closer placing a reassuring hand on his shoulder. Playfully she exclaimed.

Navi: Aaise ladayi tum phele bhi ladh chuke ho,

Aaise ladayi tum phele bhi jeet chuke ho. Toh ab ye ghabharahat kaisi?

Karan glanced at Navi, finding solace in her words. She smiled and continued

Navi: You got this Karan. You are brilliant at what you do. And, Mujh jaisi partner saath ho, Toh darne ki kya baat hai.

Due to her humorously implied words, a flicker of gratitude flashed across Karan's face, and he nodded smiling. Then, the emcee's voice boomed through the hall, cutting through the tension.

"Next up, please welcome Karan and Naviketana to the stage!"

The intensity in the room reaches its peak as all eyes turn toward Karan and Navi. They exchange a brief nod before confidently making their way towards the stage. As they step into the spotlight, the audience falls into hushed silence. Karan and Navi stand before a massive screen, ready to present their project.

The room darkens and the big screen flickered to life, illuminating their faces with a bright glow. Karan takes a deep breath, steadying his nerves, and begins speaking in a clear and confident voice. Navi's eyes shine with unwavering determination as she supports Karan, seamlessly transitioning between their well-rehearsed roles. The duo delivered a flawless performance captivating the judges and the entire audience. Their presentation was polished, innovative, and thought-provoking, leaving a lasting impact on everyone in the room. Then, applause erupts from the crowd as Karan and Navi conclude their presentation. They exchange glances, sharing a mixture of relief and excitement.

The first judge exclaimed with astonishment. "That was truly impressive! The level of detail and creativity in your project is remarkable."

The second judge nodded "Yes, I agree with you. They have clearly put in a lot of hard work and dedication. Well done guys."

The room falls into an expectant silence as the weight of the third judge's words settles over the duo. "Umm. I must say, you guys set the bar high, to be called as the best of the best. Good luck with that."

Karan and Navi feel a surge of confidence and satisfaction, knowing their dedication to work has not remained unnoticed by all judges.

Over the PA system, the emcee announces " Thank you Karan and Naviketana, for your outstanding presentation. Let's give them a huge round of applause!

The audience responded with enthusiastic clapping and cheering, showing their appreciation for the their hard work and dedication. The emcee continued, "And not just for our participants here today, but also for everyone who has contributed to this event. Your efforts are truly commendable. Let's give them all a round of applause!"

The applause swells even louder as the audience joins in, recognizing the collective dedication and passion that has made the competition a success.

"The results of this competition will be announced after 2 weeks. Until then, let the excitement and anticipation keep building. Have a good day."

The audience responded with a final round of applause. Their eagerness was visible in their expression. Karan and Navi stepped down from the stage, basking in the triumph of their performance.

Then, the scene fades out, leaving behind a lingering sense of accomplishment and the new start of their *forged friendship* that has been challenged by many obstacles.

• • •

As time triggers his pedal, both started to love hanging out and spend most of their time with each other. They are now best friends and enjoy sharing their thoughts and feelings with each other.

Everyone deserves to have a comfortable person. For Karan, we can say, Naviketana might be the one who revives him from the past fire that burned his whole innocent soul. Karan willingly keeps improving himself and he gradually overcoming the somberness he experienced a few months ago.

In addition to all of this, it brings me great joy to witness his authentic self and I hope that happiness will always be his friend. But, as I told before. life is all about ups and downs and unexpected twists and turns.

So, what's next for him? Let's find out in Chapter 5. Till then, SEE YA.

# CHAPTER V

# Trip to Madikeri

"Kartu, it's been 9 years since the day I met her... The day is still fresh in my mind. I always flinched when these words traveled through my nerves. We both stood on the balcony. But the silence made these conversations more intense. We were watching the presence of an amazing view of the sun setting down with a faded color sky. This was the day when all moments came together to meet the conclusion of this story."

• • •

Welcome back, my dear friends.

Life is meant to be flawless when it is forged through hardship and sacrifice. When a person stands still and clinches up to determine his glory, he turns out to be a different person as same as Karan does.

So, let's move in! You would find out what I meant to say.

As time travels, things started to get better between Naviketana and Karan. As he learns to share his thoughts and feelings with Navi, becoming best friends, he kept improving. However, he did not reveal anything about his past. A dark past that still battered him every time.

• • •

The day was filled with gloomy clouds, and every raindrop was marching down the steps to make a rainy vibe.

Karan and Naviketana were in the canteen and discussing their strategy for their upcoming debate competition. Ravi joins them and keeps examining the weather outside the window.

Ravi: You know what? These overcast vibes seem to convey a deep message to us.

Karan responded with a shrug, but Navi was captivated by Ravi's words. Karan confirmed this by saying,

Karan: I understand your point. I feel the same way too. I'm tired of monotony.

Ravi nodded in agreement, but before they could continue, Navi interrupted.

Navi: Hold on a second. Will you guys please stop playing these games and tell me what's going on?

Ravi exhaled and suggested,

Ravi: Relax, my sister. I was thinking we should plan a trip to appreciate the wonders of nature. What do you say?

Navi pondered for a moment before agreeing.

Navi: Hmm, that's a brilliant idea. Okay, count me in.

Ravi beams with joy and asks

Ravi: Great! So Kab chale?

A gentle voice was heard from afar.

"Can I come along for this adventure too?"

All three turned to look, but Ravi's eyes widened in surprise, and then he smiled.

Navi: Of course, Yaar. I was just thinking about you Kavi.

Ravi and Kavinayana embraced each other, and she waved at Karan and joined the conversation effortlessly.

HOLD ON!

Let me fill you in, on a small detail - Kavinayana is Ravi's girlfriend, and they have been dating past three weeks. Talking about Kavinayana, she is beautiful and a typical South Indian girl who adores her South Indian culture. Her blue eyes were stunning, but what caught most of the eyes more than anything was her shiny, flowing hair. Ravi and Kavi were a match made in heaven.

Kavi spoke up after a brief pause

Kavi: So, any ideas about destiny?

There was a lull for a few seconds until Ravi suggested.

Ravi: Tillari?

Karan: No, Yaar. We visited last year, remember?

Kavi: Jog Falls?

Navi responded with a negative.

Numerous places were suggested, but each had already been explored. Finally, Navi had the perfect location in mind, and she exclaimed,

Navi: Guys, I know a spot where we can relish the peaceful sound of raindrops and admire the panoramic scenery.

Everyone was ecstatic to hear her idea. Navi continued.

Navi: It's a place Karan has always longed to visit.

All heads nodded in agreement as the name *"Madikeri"* was uttered, causing them to erupt in excitement.

• • •

A fresh, cold breeze tickled away from her when she lowered the windows. She couldn't resist a shrug of contentment, gazing out at the magnificent mountains in front of her. Karan's gentle touch on her shoulder brought her back to reality, and she turned to meet his admiring gaze with a smile.

Karan: You seem lost.

Navi: Nature is like an addictive drug Karan, which keeps us on the edge of our minds.

Navi replied, gazing out at the lush landscape before them. Karan nodded in agreement.

Ravi: We are just 15 minutes away from our destiny. So, Yalarigu Karnatakada Swargake Swagatha

("Welcome you all to the heaven of Karnataka").

As they arrived at 7 a.m. in Galibeedu, a place nestled in the heart of Madikeri, they were greeted by a stunning natural landscape dotted with towering mountains and winding hiking trails. The sound of birds chirping and water flowing in the river, mixed with the rustling of leaves, created an immersive trekking experience that left them in awe.

Ravi: Bro! These vibes remind me of the film *"Mungaru Male."*

Karan nodded, adding,

Karan: Yeah. I agree with you. Even the film *Galipata* has the same vibe.

Ravi nodded in agreement.

Kavi bought the entrance ticket and checked all the required items for trekking.

Kavi: All checked. We're gonna start at 8 a.m. Navi, will you help me with these bags?

Navi: Yeah sure.

After making sure they had all the necessary supplies, they set off on their trek, navigating the challenging terrain with care and caution. Despite the recent heavy rainfall, they were determined to make it to the top, with Kavi and Ravi bantering and flirting along the way, while Karan and Navi engaged in easy conversation. Both were traveling with caution as they didn't want to get slipped into the muddy soil.

Navi: So, you just flipped the conversation in your favor. Didn't you?

Karan: Yeah. They have been defeated as they lack of evidence to prove their point. So, we won.

Navi: Impressive. So, I am sure you are happy to be ranked No.1 in all Belgaum debate competitions.

She said it to him with a hint of admiration in her voice. Karan was hesitant to acknowledge his achievement, instead he opting to focus on what truly mattered to him.

Karan: It's just normal stuff, Yaar. These things can't be the reason for my happiness.

Navi was intrigued by Karan's response and pressed him further.

Navi: So, what makes you happy? Mr. unpredictable.

She asked. A playful grin on her face. Karan replied as his smile grew wider as he looked at her.

Karan: YOU.

She was surprised for a moment.

Karan: You are my best friend. You know how to make me smile. You are like my *lifeline*.

Navi felt a warmth spreading through her chest at his words, her cheeks turning pink as she blushed.

Navi: Ooooo, Accha ji.

As they both were enjoying their conversing, she suddenly slipped from the edge and lost balance, on the verge of plummeting into the deep jungle below. But just in time, her hands were caught by Karan, who swiftly wrapped his arms around her back and lifted her safely on the opposite side.

Karan: You all right? Thank God I managed to hold you back.

He looked tense.

Breathless and shaken, she leaned back against a nearby tree, attempting to stand but finding it impossible due to the pain in her ankle. "My ankle!" she cried out in agony,

With concern etched on their faces, Kavi and Ravi emerged from the foliage and approached her. Karan examined her ankle, his expression growing more tense by the moment.

Karan: I need a first aid kit. Now! Ravi, woh bag de.

Karan exclaimed urgently

Ravi gets the first aid kit and Kavi comforts Navi by adjusting her to lean comfortably. Karan takes out the first aid kit

Navi: Is it broken?

She asked and looked worried, but her gaze remained fixed on Karan as he examined her ankles.

Karan: I don't think so. No need to worry, it's going to be fine.

Karan presses his palm against her foot and moves his hand side-by-side. He keeps wrapping the bandage around her ankle and Navi observes him as he looked tense and worried. She thought to herself, "He looks so concerned about me."

After finishing the bandage, Karan asked her,

Karan: It's done. We're not far from our destination. Can you make it there with my help?

She nodded with a smile.

Gratefully, Navi allowed Karan to secure his arms around her waist, gripping her arms tightly to ensure she didn't stumble or fall. Together, they pressed on towards their destination, Navi hopping along as best as she could despite the persistent ache in her ankle.

With a watchful eye, Karan kept a close eye on her every step on the way, glancing over at her periodically to check on her progress. And when the going got tough, he didn't hesitate to take action, he exclaimed suddenly.

Karan: Hold me tight.

Navi: What?

Confused, Navi barely had time to react before Karan lifted her effortlessly into his strong, muscular arms, carrying her up toward their final destination. Despite her surprise, Navi felt a wave of relief wash over her as she clung tightly to Karan. She was grateful for his steady presence and unwavering support.

Navi: I am sure you must be exhausted.

She feels concerned but she finds a mischievous glint in his eye when he admits,

Karan: Yeah of course. Lifting an overweight girl is not an easy task to complete.

Laughter broke out among all. Navi punched him playfully in the chest, laughing along with him. Despite his tease, she knew that Karan always had her back.

Karan: Ouch! Okay, I was just kidding.

Navi: That's so mean.

Finally, after a long journey, they reached the top of the sight.

The birds chirped all around from the dense jungle. Filled with cloudy weather, it started to pour. The mountains were covered in shades of many colors. However, their green color is superior among them. A river flowing down from the mountains and surrounded by woods and fields looking divine together.

All four of them spent most of their time looking at different views, exploring various sites, and enjoying every moment they spent with each other. Momentarily the evening turned out with a cold breeze. Ravi and Kavinayana decided to buy snacks from the counter while Karan decided to feel the breeze, by sitting alone on the bench. His consciousness is settled on that cold breeze, flowing around along with nature's beautiful gift right in front of him.

Navi joins in and sits next to him. Her gaze kept admiring him to find out how deep and lost he looks when he sits alone to find the unsettled answer.

Navi: Kya Soch Rahe Ho?

He turned around to meet her gaze.

Karan: Kuch Nahi Yaar. In some ways, I sometimes feel like I am the same as these mountains and trees I see all around me.

Navi: Kaise?

Karan: I feel calm, deep, and like I am lost in the woods, hoping to find the things from my past.

In order to feel the verge of this conversation, she turned around and looked at the clouds surrounding the mountain top in front of her. It looked divine and deep.

Navi: Yes, it is. Even I have found some related elements in this unrealistic scenery.

His attention turned to her. He kept looking at her to see what she had got.

She inhaled.

Navi: Nature is always concerned about its thousands of living existence that settled down within its own boundaries. Just like *how you are concerned about others.*

A blush spread across Karan's face as he folded his arms. As he had been able to find the emotions she wanted to convey.

Navi: I know. You like being surrounded by your people and taking care of them as well. Like the same way you were concerned about me today. So... I have got nothing but to convey-

When she was about to convey her gratitude, a beautiful melody surrounded them.

*Hume Tumase Pyaar Kitana,*
*Yeh Hum Nahi Jaanate.*

*Magar Jee Nahi Sakate...*
*Tumare Beena.... Aaaa.*

The pleasant and melodic voice of Kishor Kumar playing on the radio, made both of them feel these vibes, filled with the chilled breeze and fanned out in the beautiful mountains of Galibeedu. Then, she continued.

" Thank you, Karan... You brought me back to the person I used to be. A few years ago, I was lost. But now I'm myself again."

Karan looked at her, a smile playing on his lips.

"You know what Karan, this moment we are witnessing, it just feels like,

*Yeh Pal aur ye Lamha, mere Zindagi ke haseen palo me se ek hai"*

He nodded with a smile but unable to convey his feeling. Then, he turned around and folded his arms on his chest to recapture the beauty of this evening.

As the song ended, Navi gazed at Karan, feeling a strange sensation in her chest that she had never felt before. It was as though her heart was bursting with emotions she couldn't quite put her finger on. Suddenly, it dawned on her. "Is this the feeling we experience when we love someone? Am I in love with him?" she whispered to herself, unable to hide the smile that had crept onto her lips. Navi couldn't help but feel grateful for this moment. She knew that this feeling, this connection that she shared with Karan was something that she wanted to hold onto forever.

"I... I am in love with him."

# CHAPTER VI

# The Undefined Reality.

"Together, we stood in front of the portrait, the one that had captured her beauty so perfectly".

• • •

Life is just like sunrise and sunset. Whenever there is a sunrise, there is new hope, joy, and opportunity. While on the other side, a sunset refers to failure, defeat, and darkness. So, never be afraid to face any obstacles that may come in your way.

Kyunki,

"Zindagi me Muskhile kabhi Darwaza Khat-khataake nahi aati".

Hi guys! A warm welcome to all my readers. The seed of love has been planted. Will this grow enough to reward the real taste of love? It would be wonderful if the picture turns out to be into reality someday. To find out this, let's dive deeper into the oceans of this interesting journey.

*"You are my best friend. You know how to make me smile. You are my lifeline."*

These moments were constantly repeating in Navi's mind. The whole scene made her blush all the time. Although the books were kept on the table in the library, her mind was occupied with memories of him. Slowly, Kavi reached out to grab the chair in one swift motion, and with minimal effort, she quietly sat next to her. Kavi's gaze was drawn to her, and she found that Navi is lost in some beautiful sight of memories. So, she decided to take benefit from this opportunity.

Kavi: Is the prince on his way?

Navi's sub-conscious mind was still flying around in Galibeedu. In her unconscious mood, she answered Kavi's question.

Navi: Yes.

Kavi grins.

Kavi: I am sure he looks handsome and dashing.

Navi: Yes, he looks handsome and dashing.

Kavi: Is he coming towards you?

Navi: Yes. Yes, he is.

Kavi: Is he close enough?

Navi: Yes. He is really close to me.

Kavi: Is he willing kiss you?

Navi: Yes. Now he's about to kiss me. WAIT WHAT-!

Suddenly her dreams faded when Kavinayana burst into laughter. Navi dropped her forehead down and exclaimed in surprise.

Navi: "Oh no! So mean Kavi".

Kavi finds out that she was blushing.

Kavi: Awwwhh. How cute.

Navi elbows her, shaking her head.

Navi: Shut up.

Kavi: Come on don't lie to me. As you are back from your dreams, will you please tell me when this all got started?

Kavi commands. The moment Naviketana's gaze met Kavi's, she realizes Kavi won't let her go until she answers her question, which was inevitable.

Navi takes a deep breath and inhales. Kavi kept staring at her intensely.

Navi: The whole thing started last week. When we all visited Galibeedu. We had a moment to share our emotions. And you know what?

Kavi kept listening.

Kavi: Yes, go ahead.

Navi: I love the way he was concerned about me. Whenever he looks at me, he always means something with his eyes.

He loves to talk, but sometimes finds himself at a loss for words.

He loves to express himself, yet struggles to convey the right emotions

He loves to being cared for, but never reveals that he needs someone to lean on.

Despite of all this, he makes me feel delighted by everything he does and I always think about him wherever I go.

Kavi could see how happy and lost she looked. She wrapped her arms around her in a sweet hug.

Kavi: I am so happy for you dear. You both going to make a great pair. So kab Hoga ye Pyaar ka Izahar.

Navi looked a little tense.

Navi: I don't know yaar. Pehli Baar Hai, Dar Lagta hai yaar.

Her innocent answer made Kavi hug her again.

Kavi: Awwww. I love you... I love you. I love you.

Her arms were firmly gripped as she shook her whole body.

● ● ●

It's 5.30 in the evening.

"The lecturer keeps persisting the class for such a long duration. I am tired now." Navi exclaimed.

After feeling exhausted, she heads toward the college garden when someone suddenly lifts Navi and kept spinning her. She was surprised to see her boyfriend so happy. Sorry future boyfriend. And yes, it was Karan. His cute smile indicated he was delighted. She felt a spark of excitement thinking about what made Karan so excited.

Navi exclaimed.

Navi: DON'T TELL ME!

Karan: YES! WE DID IT!

He slowly releases her. She has never seen Karan so happy and excited before. Especially because of his past memories. As I have mentioned before, things were getting better...

He sighs,

Karan: We did it, Navi. We won the technical exhibition and debate. Yaar, we're both on our way to the next level. And all credit goes to you, Navi. I wouldn't have been able to complete it without you. As I told you before, *you are my life-line and you are my lucky charm*. Thanks, Navi. You literally made my day.

Her eyes were filled with light as his smile brightened them and she is filled with a sense of joy that can't be expressed in words.

In spite of the fact that he keeps telling her how he got the news and all the other stuff, Navi kept staring at him, and her heart keeps telling her, "I will always admire you. See those attractive eyes filled with a sign of bliss, which means a lot to me, Karan."

She broke out when Karan exclaimed

Karan: Navi. You seem lost-

Navi: Umm, no... I mean- I am so happy for you, Yaar. You finally did it.

Karan: Nope.

Navi: Sorry?

Karan: Learn to take credits, Yaar. *We* finally did it!

Navi: Okay, *we* finally did it. Khush?

Karan: Bohot Khush.

They both carried this joy filled with excitment

Navi: Actually, I wanted to tell you something.

Karan narrowed his eyes.

Navi: Yeah tell me, Navi.

Navi: Karan, actually..... Baat yeh hai ki...

She kept mumbling. Karan observed that she was struggling to keep her point. He embraced her and comforted her.

Karan: Itna Kya darna. Come on, just say it.

She exhales and was about to express her feelings, suddenly Ravi jumped on Karan and brushed his hair.

Ravi: Maccha!! Congratulations! You both made it!!

Ravi offered a group hug with his both hands open. They both accepted and were ready for a group hug when Kavi comes around and adjusts herself into joining them all.

Kavi: You can't have a group hug without *meeee*.....

They nodded with a laugh. Then they wrapped their arms around each other for the group hug.

When they parted ways, Karan exclaimed.

Karan: Let's have something. Here's a treat from my end.

All get cheered up.

While Navi kept walking with Karan, her feet trembled on the spur of the moment and her body falls straight into Karan's arms.

" Aay hay". Kavi nods when she turns and finds the filmy scene rolling away. On the other side, Navi kept looking at him when he lifts her back toward him.

Karan: I've seen you for a while now. You seem to be lost somewhere. Kiske yaado me kho jaati ho?

She starts blushing and turns back and whispers
"Tumare".

Karan: Sorry?

Her eyes went wide open when she turned around.

She felt startled when he replied.

Navi: Did you hear what I said?

He had a pause in his conversation. Her heart was pounding in her chest.

Karan: Of course not. That's why I asked.

She exhales.

Navi: Thank God. I am all right don't worry. Ab Chal na badi bhuk lagi hai.

Karan: Aare, badi ajeeb ladaki hai. Okay. Let's go.

There was a smile shared between the two, and then everyone walked to the canteen.

• • •

Time kept rolling around.

Despite trying to find the right time to express her feelings, she was unable to do so.

The end of college life was near for the students and they were ecstatic for the final Prom dance of their college years. All were excited to make their move, spend their indelible night with their partner, and create flourishing memories to remember.

The only person who kept himself away from these things and spent all his time in the library was him. There was nothing he loved more than keeping himself busy in the world full of books.

Yes, I am talking about Karan.

His conscious mind came out of his world when he glanced up to see a beautiful face. She kept admiring him, and the smile on her face made him feel delighted.

Navi: You are coming with me.

After a moment, he realized and attempted to obstruct.

Karan: No. Don't even think that I will ever come to prom. I don't like it.

Navi's expression turned out to be downcast.

Navi: Oh come on! It's your final year. I want you to have fun. Chal na!

Karan breathes out and grabs her palms.

Karan: Navi, you know how uncomfortable I feel there? It makes me sick. You should join Ravi and Kavinayana, yaar. After the party, we'll both have dinner together. Sounds good?

She takes her hand back and looked disappointed.

Navi: Okay. Don't come with me. I won't go either.

She turns back and was ready to leave.

Karan immediately blows out to stop her. He stands in front of her and blocks her path.

Karan: Navi, you are blackmailing me.

Navi: Jo samjhna hai samjho. Aur tume kya me jau ya na jau.

She tried to avoid him and was about to leave. But she suddenly stopped. When she turned back, he held her hands. He spins her and whispers.

Karan: *I am coming.*

Navi: Be loud. I can't hear you.

He smiled coquettishly

Karan: Okay, fine. Navi, I am coming for prom.

Navi's delighted face made him smile.

Karan: Badi Daramebaaz ho yaar.

Navi: I will take that as a compliment.

Karan: What?? Really.

After a funny pause, they burst into laughter.

• • •

Today, this evening is set to witness something that has never happened before. Karan with a smooth spade beard was waiting for someone. His graceful blue suit were a source of amusement and charm.

Finally, his gaze gleamed up when he finds the one he was waiting for.

Her curly and shiny hair were bouncing on her shoulder. When she flips around her beautiful hair, he finds the hidden moon that appeared in front of him that lights up this decent night.

Who says we won't find *Rambe and Urvashi on Earth?*

She looks stunning and divine in her long blue dress embellished with golden petals of flowers.

Karan was lost for a moment in the shade of her beauty. Every step she takes down the stairs feels like petals falling from heaven. Despite his best efforts, he could not figure out what this feeling meant to him.

Navi: So, kaisi lag rahi hu?

He didn't reply. Being lost, he kept looking at her.

Navi: Karan?

The moment she shakes him, puts her hand on his shoulder, and asks him again, then he comes back to the real world.

He shakes his head and begins to stutter.

Karan: Yeah... um. I mean..

She slowly moves forward and keeps looking at him.

Navi: Relax. Now tell me. Kaisi lag rahi hu?

After taking a step back, he pointed at the moon with his fingers.

Karan: Us Chand Ko dekh rahi ho?

"Ha, dekh rahi hu" she said.

Karan: Bheleyi Chand us Aasaman me ho. Lekin usaki Chandani aaj meri samane hai.

Navi: Aaay-Haay. How cheesy.

She starts blushing as she tangles her hair.

As they stared at each other for a long time, the moment settled into a long pause. But Karan broke the momentum by saying.

Karan: Umm. I think we should leave now. Kavinayana and Ravi are waiting for us.

Navi nodded in agreement. But the momentum built in that short period of time made her blush and she felt felicitous to be lost in someone she loved.

The college is just 15 minutes away from her apartment so they decided to walk. When they arrived, they were astonished to look around the campus. People are filled with joy and happiness.

"Hey look I found her". Kavi said in excitement.

Karan and Navi turn around when Ravi and Kavinayna walk toward them.

Kavi: My dear, you look like an angel!

Kavi hugged Naviketana and exclaimed. But she was amazed to see Karan.

Kavi: That's awesome to see my bro participating in this promp. Welcome to our kind of stuff Bro.

Karan shook his head. But he kept admiring Kavinayana.

Karan: Ravi. Did you see that?

Ravi: See what?

Ravi looks curious.

Karan swelled with pride as he gazed upon Kavinayana, adorned in a breathtaking typical South Indian lehenga. With a gentle lift of her chin, he found the words to express his admiration for her stunning attire.

Karan: Did you see my sister, How divine and beautiful she looks in her typical lehenga. It truly reflects your grace and elegance, my dear sister.

Kavi's voice grew quiet and her eyes flicked to see Karan. With her arms out to embrace him, she leaned slightly toward his chest. Then she admits

Kavi: Awhh. Thanks, Bhai. So sweet of you. I am delighted with your words.

Ravi nodded.

Then, they all headed to an attractive sight with a group of people dancing, drinking, and having a good time. There is a piece of party music playing around. They all kept embracing their friends while Karan and Ravi moved to greet other acquaintances, while Kaviyana and Navi opted to perch at the counter.

But, there was a moment when Karan's attention was drawn back to his past when the music turned out with the words,

*"Is kadar pyaar hai, tumase hai hum safar"*.

A massive wave of feelings dispersed, and each feeling carried something different. Some waves are of happiness. Later, there are some waves of sadness and anger as well. Lastly, some waves are filled with tears and betrayals.

The rage keeps building in him and he is tempted to get fresh air so he leaves. Far across the counter, Navi observes the whole change in Karan. She denied the drink offered by Kavi and rushed toward Karan but Ravi interrupted standing in front of her.

Ravi: Navi, wait.

His voice was tensed.

Navi: But why? He just left the party. What's the matter?

Ravi: There's something he doesn't like when anyone gets involved in it. Let him face it. I assure you he will come back.

Ravi try to convince her. But she looked sad and disappointed.

Then, Navi cautiously approached Karan as he was making his way toward the back door. Concern etched on her face, she inquired, "Karan, what happened? Why are you leaving like this?"

Karan, his emotions raw and tumultuous, responded sternly, "Navi, please leave me alone for a while."

Persistently, she probed, "What's the matter?"

Karan's reply came as a firm command, "Navi, kuch baate andhero ki saaye jaise hothi hai jo baya nahi kiye jaati. So please, *leave me alone.*"

She was shocked and stand stir for a moment. She said to herself

"What happened to him. Why he didn't tell me what was going on with him?"

Her disappointment brought her to the bar counter. She sighs heavily and runs her hand through her hair. Still, she kept wondering what this was all about. She was seriously stressed out and didn't know what to do. So, she decided to get a drink to drown her sorrows.

"Two Bacardi and soda, please," she exclaimed.

She was presented with a glass filled with soda and two Bacardi by the bartender.

As she kept repeating the order, she kept rolling. She was only trying to build herself up so she could tell him what she felt.

Meanwhile, Karan was standing quiet and lost in his own thoughts in the garden. He kept looking at the dark and deep sky that has blended into this evening.

He finds a firm squeeze on his shoulder. When he turned around he finds.

"Is there a reason why you didn't tell me about this?"

His gaze shifted to Navi as he was unsettled to see her in such a situation. She kept stumbling and her eyes had turned red. But still, he could see the depth of her dark eyes. It's how intense and deep it looks as if they want to express something really important to him.

Karan: have u drunk? You shouldn't do....

Navi interrupts

Navi: Shhhhhhh.

Navi moves forward and with slight pressure, she holds his palm.

Navi: You literally had no idea Karan how much it's killing me that you haven't told me what's going on with you. Are you even aware that I attended this party just for *you*?

Karan: I...I am sorry Navi. I...

She interrupts again.

Navi: No... You totally forgot. So what did you do? You *just left*.

He was quiet for a moment but Navi had no control at all.

Navi: So, I needed this. The only way I can stop pretending is to have alcohol. I have held this damn feeling for too long. Now, it's difficult for me to hold on to this anyway. Karan, I walked a long distance in order to expel my feelings.

He looked confused. She gazed up looking straight at him.

Navi: Karan. I want to tell you something that's really, really important.

She wouldn't be able to stand and Karan wrapped his arms around her so that she wouldn't fall. He knows that she hasn't fully recovered from her injury.

She kept laughing in a sarcastic manner. A smile spread across her face, and a huge emotion passed through her mind.

Navi: You are my best friend, right? Don't you?

He keeps holding her back and he looks tensed

Karan: Navi. You don't know what you're talking so let's get out of here.

A sudden exclamation escaped her lips as she squeezed his suit to stop him.

Navi: Noo! I don't give a shit about other stuff.

Tell me first, you are my best friend, right? You...are.

She slurred; Karan keeps reassuring her by saying

Karan: Yeah Navi. I am your best friend. Now come on let's get out of here. Tum hosh me nahi ho.

Her voice keeps growing louder.

Navi: No! We are not going anywhere. This day...this day will witness the *dark truth* I want to share. And you are the victim, Karan.

Gradually, her eyes started filling with tears.

Her vision keeps fading away but she persists in her determination to express the damn thing.

"You're the only one who really understands Karan"

She buried her face in his arms. He could feel the warmth rushing toward him. She wrapped her arms around his neck.

This was intense. The emotions they were experiencing can be felt by both of them. Her face caught his attention and he dropped his eyes.

He knows lots of things are vague to understand. But today it might appear as a mirror. Karan observes that she keeps fading away but she still murmurs something.

She was quiet for a short time and suddenly, she groaned.

She starts sobbing which makes her break out really hard from inside. She feels the pain she suffered many years ago is hurting her now as if she were stabbed by a thousand knives piercing her inner feelings. Now, the wounds she had begun to hurt again. Tears kept rolling down her cheeks.

Navi: I still remember the day, Karan. And it still makes me feel terrified. It was my 12<sup>th</sup> birthday. The happiest day of my life. Soon, turned out to be the cruelest nightmare that ever happened in my life. The vision I saw that day, It still looks so real whenever I imagined it.

She starts gasping. Gradually it becomes more intense with every breath she takes. Karan holds her arms to comfort her. But the emotions she's carrying at the moment are really making him feel worried.

Navi: It's full of BLOOD. It gets splattered down the street. I...I can see the car burning. The bodies were everywhere. U know... U know Karan...

Now, her expression starts scaring him. Her eyes turned red like tears of red blood pouring around her and witnessing her immense pain. She was filled with fear and agony.

Navi: I had seen them. I had seen... My mom and dad lay there. They were covered in blood. The whole body is covered with full of BLOOD. I HAVE SEEN THEM DEAD. They didn't make it Karan. They didn't..I...It just keeps replaying the entire scene in my head..

Her expression is filled with extreme pain. She starts bawling and sobbing.

Tears streamed down his cheeks... He literally had no idea what to do.

Karan: I am... I am sorry Navi. Life was so hard on you... I.. I swear, I will be with you. *I am always with you...*

He hugs her again...

The pain gets suppressed by his pleasing words...his heart beats like a bullet and he keeps yelling "Navi, you won't suffer this again!"

There was a long pause, and that was the moment she realized.

Finally, the fateful moment has arrived. Karan is aware that her eyes are about to reveal something that he barely grasps. The moonbeams were privy to this moment of emotion. Even her subconscious mind admitted, "This is the moment I have been waiting for. Let me express my sentiments. For if I don't, I may never see you again, *my love*". Her heartbeat quickened, and she made her move.

*"Karan...you know I cannot survive without you. The moments we spent together were pure bliss."*

Navi admits once more to herself.

A tear rolled down her cheek, and the scene faded into obscurity.

"Karan, I Lo-..."

Just then, Ravi interjected.

"My apologies for the interruption, Karan. I was here to tell you that they've got into an accident..."

She falls on him and Karan wraps her around...then his attention turns to Ravi...

Karan: Who met with the accident?

He could observe Ravi's voice was rumbling.

Karan: *Raviii. Tell me who the hell Got Hurt. Just Say It...*

Karan starts yelling in tension.

Ravi shoots desperately

Ravi: Karan, Gayatri, and her mother have been injured in the car accident and they are in the hospital. Gayatri just keeps telling your name when she wakes up... I think we should leave... *Now*

Karan was stunned by the news that he just heard...his mind was blank and didn't know what to do...

Then he quickly springs into action, scooping up Navi and rushing her to her apartment with Kavinayana and Ravi following closely behind reaching out to the apartment.

Once there, he gently laid her on the bed.. she was still murmuring something that was barely audible. He kept staring at her for a moment then kissed her forehead and said.

Karan: I will be coming back for you, Navi...I will be coming back very soon...

When he was about to leave, he noticed his hand was seized by Navi.

Navi: Don't... Don't go away... I need you. I can't be without you.

She uttered in a slurred voice.

Karan: I will be there with you...for now, you just need some sleep... He slowly slackens her palms before he leaves.

Then he found Ravi explaining to Kavi what had happened. When Karan was about to say something, Kavi interrupted

Kavi: You don't have to say anything Bhai. Don't worry, I'll take care of her...you have to be quick and take care of yourself...

They both nod and left...

● ● ●

We don't know what's going to happen next...

# CHAPTER VII

# The Realization.

Ravi and Karan have been rushed to the hospital to find Gayatri and her mom. As Ravi looks over at the old lady sitting in the waiting room, he finds someone familiar sitting next to her...

It's *Gayatri*.

To his surprise, her head was wrapped in bandages and her face was pale and unreadable...There was no expression at all on her face.

Karan wasn't able to react when his gaze found Gayatri... As he is relieved that she is okay, but it instantly reflects back on the day...the day that he was been stabbed by her.

As Gayatri turns around, she sees Karan standing straight in front of her. Her gaze is fixed on him as she stands up. Karan could see the sorrow in her eyes.

Slowly she moves towards Karan. But Suddenly,

Karan: Stop! Stay away from me

He commands.

She stopped. Unable to react, then she takes a deep breath and speaks

Gayatri: I know. You never gonna accept that. That you just came for me.

He was in no mood to listen to her words. Ravi glanced in her direction.

Karan: Please don't think I came for you. You know what? I don't even give a shit about you! I am just here for your mom. She is the only person who is not like you.

Her lips were sealed for a moment. But then, she tried to confess

Gayatri: Karan. It's been 4 years since I've been with you. Unfortunately, I was the one who made that mistake...and I couldn't repair it. But still, I know you care about me. And...

She had a pause. The tension between them keeps mounting.

Karan: Enough!

Gayatri takes a step forward and keeps facing him straight. There is something that matters to her that she wants to confess to.

Gayatri: Karan, accept it. Today, I just want to talk to you and you can't deny that fact.

"Gayatri, that's enough"

He grabs her arms and pushes away, unable to forgive her for the pain she caused him. His eyes start glistening with anger.

Karan: Now you feel sorry for what you did! The only thing you know to hurt people and...

But then, the situation turned upside down Until she yells in the moment of shocking revelation.

"Stop! Karan. For the sake of God listen to me... *Abhi and my mom are no more!*"

This revelation finally grabbed Karan's attention and allowed Gayatri to explain everything. He loosen his grip and stunned for a moment when the word hits.

"Please listen to me," she said with tears streaming down her cheeks..

Ravi convinces Karan to listen to her and figure out what actually happened. As a result, Karan decided to have this conversation in a suitable environment.

Gayatri and Karan sat on a bench, a short distance apart. Ravi, who had been watching from a distance, decided to leave them alone, giving them the space they needed to resolve their issues. Both were lost deep in their memories. But it was Gayatri who finally made the first move, breaking the silence with a voice that was barely above a whisper.

Gayatri: You know what? I realized today that Karma is a real thing. God made me pay for what I did in my past, and my ego slammed out at a person whom I'm supposed to be praised like anything. He took care of me, he was honest with me for the past 4 years, and he loves *me and my family*. It was me who always compared and judged your love and honesty. I never knew the true love of a family. Whenever I thought about you, I always imagined that you had to choose between your family and me. But now, here I am. Lost my own *family*. Lost my own reason to live. At a young age, I lost my dad, and now I have lost my mother as well. Now, nothing left me. *I think I really deserve this.*"

Karan remained speechless, consumed by his anguish. The waves crashing on the shore failed to distract him from the weight of her words. Meanwhile, he tried to meet her gaze by flipping his eyes.

But he felt broken when he saw her sorrowful and regretful eyes.

Even gayatri keep looking at him. She knew what he is feeling .

Gayatri: Me janti hu, tum kya soch rahai ho.

He keeps looking at her.

Gayatri: Karan

He just not able to resemble, so he replied with,

Karan: Hmm.

Gaytri: mujhe pata hai, *jo kuch bhi maine kiya woh maafi ke layak nahi..*

Her plea for forgiveness was met with a heavy heart. But still, he doesn't want to respond.

As she stares at him, she gently places her hands on his palms.

Gaytri: lekin, ho saake toh mujhe maaf kar dena, Karan. Today, I want to tell you, tum ek acche aur sacche insaan ho. Remember, you always told me that whenever you close your eyes, you're gonna find the people whom you love the most.

She paused and kept looking at him in hopes that at least he had responded to her soreness words. But he won't. She swallows hard and made her statement.

"When I close my eyes, *I still find you. I still find you,* Karan. That's how special you are because your presence makes people get to realize what they want. And that makes how important you are."

He kept his emotions suppressed.

That's when she realized it he never gonna response. There was an unsatisfied smile on her face.

With a heavy heart, she rose to her feet, casting one last tearful glance at Karan before uttering her final words.

"Goodbye, Karan."

And with that, she departed.

Karan remained motionless for a long time, arms folded and his back against the bench, attempting to process the recent events. He felt drained and emotionally broken. Tears keeps rolling down his cheeks once she left. The eyes filled with tears was the only painful emotion left which finally tends to be released. After a long silence, he drowned out with all the pain suppressed in him and decided to keep himself strong.

He kept looking at the dark sky before closing his eyes.

As he shut his eyes, a vivid image began to materialize in his mind's eye - a stunning young woman descending the grand staircase, her flowing gown draped gracefully around her form. With each passing moment, the details of her appearance became clearer and more vibrant, from the shimmering fabric of her dress to the delicate curve of her cheeks. When he caught sight of the beauty before him, a smile tugged at the corners of his lips.

But just as quickly as the dream had begun, it came to an abrupt end. As he realized the identity of the girl in his fantasy dream, his eyes shot open with a jolt, dispelling the illusion and returning him to reality. He just can't believe it. It was *Naviketana!* the object of his unrequited affection, and the *realization* of this fact left him feeling both elated and disheartened all at once.

"What was that?" He yelled.

For a moment, he was lost in a sea of conflicting emotions.

Karan: Why did I have a vision of Naviketana?. What does that actually mean?

After a few moment when he realizing what that meant, he was stunned because he had just realized something he had heard just a few moments ago.

"Remember, you always told me that whenever you close your eyes, you're gonna find the people whom you love the most"

Karan: No. It's not possible at all. How can I...

He had never experienced anything like it before, and the sheer intensity of his feelings left him gasping for air.

Karan: If this were the reality, why did I not feel this way before?

He closed his eyes again for a while.

He still finds her beautiful vision coming to his mind.

Karan: I think it is.

She was the one who brought me back from Death Valley.

She was the one who made me always smile.
She was the one who made me *be myself.*
She was the one who
I LOVE.
How dumb I was.

He can't stop what was this feeling? But he knew he is in love.

As he pondered what to do next, his mind raced with a thousand different possibilities. "Should I confess my love for her? Or should I keep my feelings to myself?"

The answer came to him with sudden clarity. The only feeling he had now been to confess his emotion. The scene keeps fading with his final words.

"I had to tell her what I felt about her. Chahe kuch bhi ho jaye"

• • •

The sky turned into shade to witness this moment and the first drops of rain started to sprinkle down. Karan's heart was racing with anticipation. He took a deep breath and gathered the courage to tell Navi how he truly felt.

He informed Kavinayana, asking her to deliver a message to Navi, requesting that she meet him in the park.

Finally, he saw Navi approaching, and his heart skipped a beat. Their eyes met, and for a moment, time seemed to stand still as they both gazed at each other in anticipation.

Even though he tried to roll his eyes as it was making him nervous, she still kept looking at him.

She looked tense. Tears filled her eyes, which made to feel him more intense.

In order to comfort her, he drew himself closer and placed his hands on her shoulders.

"Navi...."

But before Karan could speak further, Navi interrupted him.

"Wait,"

She said it softly

"Mujhe Bhi kuch kehna hai"

Drawing closer to him she hugged him, whispered something, and then,

She just *left*...

Just like that, Karan stood there in shock, replaying her words in his head. Trying to make sense of what had just happened.

And you know what?

That was the last day he met Naviketana Maheshwari. *Ever.*

CHAPTER VIII

# Naviketana

*9 years later.*

Last night, I landed in Belagavi from Delhi. And my first act was to grab my phone and text Karan that I had just arrived in Belagavi. He was astonished by my arrival and promised to be at the airport within a few minutes. As I kept waiting for Karan, I took out my phone to inform my wife of my safe arrival. And I informed her that I would be returning to Delhi in 2 days. Talking about my dear friend Karan, today, he is working as the CEO of India's largest hydraulic company, THE ORINE PRIVATE LIMITED. And for me, it always feels a pleasure to come back to Belagavi. Namma Preetiya Belagavi. (My lovely Belagavi)

As I was checking my emails and other stuff, I looked up as he called my name and saw Karan approaching. His eyes were filled with joy, and his face was beaming with happiness and emotion.

Karan rushed towards me and wrapped me in a tight embrace. I felt a rush of emotions overwhelm me, and I couldn't help but feel grateful for this moment.

Really, I feel a warm sense of joy emanating from this hug.

"Mere dost, teri bohot yaad aayi," I said

Karan held my shoulders and said,

"I am so happy to see you back, Kartu. I just can't express it."

I kept watching Karan's reaction closely, feeling my own emotions bubble to the surface.

"Kaisa hai yaar?" I asked.

Karan replied with excitement.

"Sab thik hai. Tu bata Anitha Bhabhi kaisi hai aur hamari Aradhya kaisi hai?"

"Sab maze me hai"

I replied, feeling a sense of relief and joy wash over him.

Karan hugged me again with pride, conveying his excitement in the most gentle way.

"Come, let's go," he said, leading me to his bungalow.

After a long journey, I was exhausted and needed rest. But my heart was filled with joy and happiness at the reunion with my dear friend.

As I lay on the bed, I looked around the room. Everything felt familiar, yet it was different. I closed my eyes, took a deep breath, and let myself relax.

• • •

It was 7 in the morning. The sun's rays kept falling from the shades of the falling leaves. I found myself lost in the blissful sight of children playing and enjoying their games on the streets, and I kept admiring from the balcony. Then a cold breeze swept by, carrying with it the weight of past memories. Those memories connected Karan from his past.

I turned around and glanced when Karan arrived with a tray, holding a tea set.

"Tea?" he offered, to which I replied with an eager nod.

With a gentle smile, he poured a steaming cup and stirred in some sugar before handing it to me. His eyes wandered over to the portrait in the room, its beauty illuminating every corner. He stood in front of the portrait and took a sip and a deep sigh followed

"Kartu, it's been 9 years since *the day I met her* in the park... The day is still fresh in my mind."

He said, his voice laced with hidden feelings. Just as the ocean may flow peacefully on the banks, but still, the waves have something deep to convey.

"I remember," I said, acknowledging his words.

"It was the last time you saw Naviketana Maheshwari."

He nodded in agreement, picking up his cup once more.

" Later she got married" I pointed out.

A silence hung in the air as he stared down at the floor, lost in his thoughts.

"That day I was stunned to hear what she said. She came closer and whispered."

He felt that moment for a while and then continued

*"Can you tolerate me for the rest of your life if you marry me? I am sure you will. Because you have no other option. I will keep waiting for your reply, Karan.* She said that and just left.

He paused for a moment and continued

"Since then, she has been called *Mrs. Chauhan*," he said but interrupted with my words.

" Yes. *Mrs. Naviketana Karan Chauhan*". I said in agreement.

A gentle smile appeared on his face as he turned to face me.

Then, he took another sip before walking towards his showcase, where he opened an old wooden box and pulled out a golden locket.

" You know what, Kartu? There are times when memories are more precious than people. like this locket."

He paused, lost in thought before continuing.

"She gifted me this last year. I was so happy and excited. She..."

His words became jumbled, and he repeated them again, his eyes widening with each passing moment and his expression filled with *pain*. "She... this... this was..."

His voice trailed off, his thoughts consumed by bittersweet recollection. He shook his head, lost in reverie. Suddenly, his eyes widened with a fresh realization.

" Yes, she... she gave me this before she *left me*" he kept saying this

"Yes. She gave me this before she *passed away*. It was the last gift she ever gave me." His voice cracked, tears streaming down his face.

"This was the last thing she ever gave me before she left me due to *cancer*."

His sobs grew louder and more intense, and he sank to his knees, clutching the locket to his chest. My heart ached for him, but I knew that his heartache would remain with him for the rest of his life, when she passed away.

His sobs filled the room, and I felt a range of emotions flood over me. I moved to his side, offering comfort and support as he clung to my arm. "Please," he said between sobs. "Don't stop me today. I want to share this pain with someone I believe in."

He continued to sob, his voice hoarse and ragged.

"I was holding her when she took her last breath, Kartu. I watched her fade away from me, helpless to do anything to save her." His anguish was palpable, and I felt my own tears welling up in sympathy.

He lifted his head and looked at me. His eyes were red and swollen.

" Karan, I am with you brother. I am always be your side"

I listened to him in silence and presented my words to him. But still, my heart ached for him. As he clung to me, and I held him tight for a moment I offered what comfort I could, and after a time, the tears began to subside, and the room fell in silence.

• • •

As the sun rose the next morning, birdsong filled the air, and leaves fell gently from the trees, drifting down to earth like memories from the past. All that was left were those memories. A collection of memories, both good and bad.

Together, we stood in front of the portrait, the one that had captured her beauty so perfectly. Yes, it is Navi whom we keep admiring in the portrait. And her presence could still be felt even though she was no longer with us. As we gazed at the painting, a soft touch landed on our shoulders. When we turned around, we felt a sense of remembrance when we saw them for the first time in a long time. *It's Ravi and Kavinayana.* A happy married couple.

Both smiled softly at us..

"My sister was so adorable," Ravi whispered with a hint of sadness in his voice.

"Yes, she was. And she was *my angel.*" Kavinayana nodded in agreement but tears kept rolling down her cheeks.

As the morning wore on and the day began to unfold, we simply stood there, gazing at the portrait and remembering. Together, we reminisced about the memories we had shared with Navi, reliving the moments that had brought us all so much joy. The world seemed to fade away, leaving us with nothing but memories that we held so dear.

As the moment came to an end, we all shared a satisfied smile, grateful for the time we had spent together and the memories that would stay with us forever...

• • •

Lekin, you may begin with a question whispered deep in your heart. Many Unanswered question have still left.

So,

Yeh kahani abhi adhuri hai,

Kuch baato ko janana bada zaruri hai.

Mushkilo ko paar karke pyaar ko paya toh ja sakta hai,

Magar, usi pyaar ko,

Kahi mushkilo ko baad bhi na bacha paye,

Toh Oo khuda bhi lachar ho jata hai.

Khushiyo ke un haseen palo ke baad jab gham darwaza khat-khatathi hai,

Sach kehta hu mere dost,

Ek bar koi is duniya se chala jaye toh uski baadi yaad aati hai.

There are a lot of things to be shared along with hidden emotions that are suppressed by the lost pieces of puzzles.

You have seen how love is pure to its own extent.

But now, You're able to discover how love can endure beyond life and death.

Coming for you, Soon

**"THE DAY YOU LEFT ME"**